Card Games

for Kids

TERRY EAGLE

ReD
KiTE

This edition published and distributed in the UK by
Red Kite Books,
an imprint of Haldane Mason Ltd
PO Box 34196, London NW10 3YB

Reprinted 2002

First published in 2000

ISBN: 1-902463-81-1

A HALDANE MASON BOOK

Art Director: Ron Samuel
Editor: Jane Ellis
Design: Zoë Mellors
Artwork: Samantha Bale

Printed in China

Contents

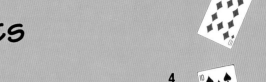

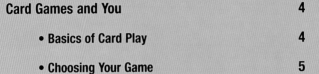

Card Games and You

Ever been bored in the car or coach, on a train or plane, or even at home? You have the solution right in your hands! Card games are not only tremendous fun, they can help you learn about numbers, work out plans, and solve problems.

In this book you will find a whole range of different card games for you to play with one or more partners. Some are very simple games that you can play with younger children, others are games you can play with adults. You'll find that they all have one thing in common – great entertainment.

Basics of Card Play

The pack: A standard pack of cards has 52 cards, divided into four suits of 13 cards each. Each suit is clearly marked by its own symbol – hearts, clubs, diamonds and spades. Each card has a value. Ace is always either top or bottom, depending on the game. Then, from the top, the order is king, queen, jack, and the number cards from 10 to 2. There is an extra card, the joker, which is not used in the games in this book. (When the joker is used, you can give him

any value you want. If you lose a card from the pack, the joker can stand in for it.)

Shuffling and cutting: At the start of every game, unless the rules say otherwise, the pack is shuffled. This means mixing the cards so that no one can tell what order they are in. It takes practice to become a skilful shuffler. To cut the pack after it has been shuffled, get another player to lift about half of the shuffled pack, and place that half underneath, so that the upper half of the pack becomes the lower half.

Cutting and drawing for dealer: Cutting for dealer is letting each player in turn cut the pack to show a card. Drawing is when each player draws a card from the pack. Normally the player with the highest card wins, although in some games it is the

lowest. If it is a tie, the players involved try again.

Dealing: Always deal from the top of the pack. Slide the top card slightly forward with your thumb, take it between forefinger and thumb of the other hand, and place it face down before the player, starting with the player to your left, and dealing to yourself last. Players should not pick up their hands until all the cards needed for the game have been dealt.

Choosing Your Game

Some card games are very straightforward and others are more tricky. Also, different people pick up rules and techniques at varying speeds. As a very general guide, the games in this book have been given an easier/harder rating. A single * indicates Easy, and two ** means Harder. But all the games in the book should be well within your scope, even if you have never played before.

Games for

2

or more
players

Beggar My Neighbour *

Also known as Beat Your Neighbour Out of Doors.
Number of Players: Two.
How to Win: By ending up holding all 52 cards.

How to Do It:

Use the standard 52-card pack.
Cut for dealer (higher card).
Shuffle the cards and deal them
all out, one at a time, face down.

The other player must then pay out the
proper number of cards, one at a time,
face up:

Ace – four cards
King – three cards
Queen – two cards
Jack – one card

If all the cards put down for payment
are number cards, the player who put
down the ace or picture card now picks
up the pile and puts it at the bottom of
his stack. This is how cards are won. If
one of the payment cards turns out to
be an ace or picture card, the payment
stops and the other player must
immediately pay out the correct
number of cards to his opponent. This
can continue for some time.

The non-dealer turns
over the top card
from his pile. If it is a
number card (from 2
to 10), the dealer
covers it with a card
from the top of his
pile. Cards continue
to be put down in this
way until one player
puts down an ace,
king, queen or jack.

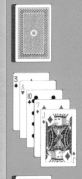

Player 2 turned over an ace –
requiring four payment cards.
However, his opponent's third
payment card is a jack, so player
2 now has to pay one card.

Eventually, one
player will turn up
only number cards
in payment, and
then the pile will be
lost to his opponent!

◆◆◆◆◆◆◆◆◆◆◆◆◆◆◆◆◆◆◆◆◆◆◆◆◆◆◆◆◆◆◆◆

Catch the Ten *

This game is often called Scotch Whist.

Number of players: Two to seven.

How to Win: By winning tricks, especially with the top five cards of the trump suit.

How to Do it:

1 Reduce the number of cards in your pack to 36, by taking out all cards between 2 and 5. If there are five or seven players, take out one of the 6s to make a 35-card pack. Aces count as high, so the range goes from ace down to 6.

2 Cut for dealer (highest card). Deal out all the cards, one at a time The dealer turns up the final card to show trumps, before taking it into his own hand.

3 The player on the dealer's left leads, and other players, from the left, must follow suit if they can. If you cannot follow suit, you can play a trump card or any other card.

4 The trick is won by the highest card of the suit led, or by the highest trump. The winner of a trick leads to the next.

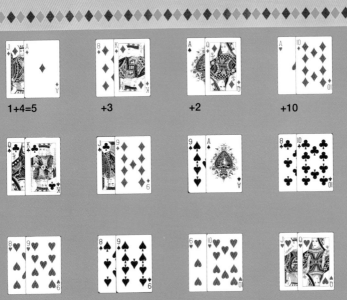

1+4=5   +3   +2   +10

Diamonds are trumps in this hand. Here are the tricks won by a player after one hand, in a two-player game. He wins 20 points for his trumps, plus 6 points because he has six more cards than the 18 he was originally dealt.

Scoring:

The top five cards in the trump suit are: ace (4); king (3); queen (2); jack (1) and 10 (10). No other cards have value. When all tricks are taken, each player counts the value of the trumps in his set of tricks, and also adds one point for every card he now has in addition to the cards he was originally dealt. The first player to reach a score of 41 wins (this will normally take several hands).

Card Games for Kids

Gin Rummy **

You need: 52-card pack, and score sheets for each player.
Number of Players: Two.
How to Win: To build up a winning hand of melds and be first to score 100 points.

How to Do It:

Cut for dealer (higher card wins). Note that aces are low in this game. Dealer shuffles, and deals ten cards, one at a time, to each player. The remaining cards are placed face down on the table to form the stock. The top card of the stock is turned face up by the dealer, and placed by itself, to start the discard pile.

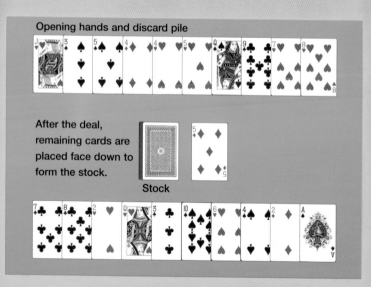

Opening hands and discard pile

After the deal, remaining cards are placed face down to form the stock.

Stock

10

The non-dealer has picked up the 5 diamonds from the discard pile and put down the 9 clubs from his hand. He can now make a meld of three 5s.

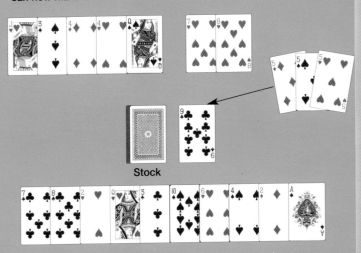

Stock

The non-dealer can choose to take up this card, or refuse it; he cannot draw a card from the stock pile. If he refuses it, the turn goes to the dealer. If the dealer also refuses the turned-up card (in card language, he says 'pass') the other player can now take the top (face-down) card from stock.

Whenever a player picks up a card, he must also discard one from his hand (the card that has just been picked up can be the one that is discarded, if it is no use).

◆◆◆◆◆◆◆◆◆◆◆◆◆◆◆◆◆◆◆◆◆◆◆◆◆◆◆◆◆◆◆

3 The aim is to be the first to go out by laying down all your cards in melds (sets of three or more cards of the same suit in consecutive numbers, counting from ace as low; or sets of three or more cards from different suits but with the same value).

If you can get rid of all the cards in your hand by fitting them into melds, call out 'Gin!' or knock on the table. You receive a bonus of 25 points plus the value of your opponent's unmelded cards.

You can also choose to go out if you have some melds, and the unmelded cards in your hand have a value of ten points or less. In this case, however, your opponent has the chance to 'lay off' any of his own unused cards on your melds, and to add to his own melds using your unmelded cards, before the score is counted.

4 The player with the lower value of unmelded cards receives a 25-point bonus. If neither player has gone out before the last two cards are drawn from the stock, the round is treated as a no-score draw.

Scoring

Court cards (king, queen, jack): ten points each. Ace: one point. Number cards: as their number value. The value of the unmatched or unmelded cards still in your hand counts against you. If the player who went out has the same, or greater value of remaining cards as his opponent, the opponent gets a ten-point bonus plus the difference between the card values.

The winner of the game is the first to reach 100 points.

Stock

Examples of some different melds put down during a game.
Remember, players can add cards to an opponent's melds.

Go Boom *

Number of Players: *Two to six.*
The Aim: *To be first to get rid of all one's cards.*

How to Do It:

Use the standard pack of 52 cards. Cut for dealer (highest card). The dealer deals seven cards, one at a time, to each player. The rest of the pack is placed face down and forms the stock.

The non-dealer, or first player to the dealer's left, leads. The next player must follow suit, or play a card of the same face value as the lead (aces are high). All other players must follow the suit or match the value of the last card.

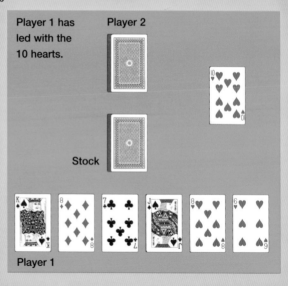

Player 1 has led with the 10 hearts.

Player 2

Stock

Player 1

Player 2 cannot follow suit or match the lead card, so he must pick up from the stock until he can play a card.

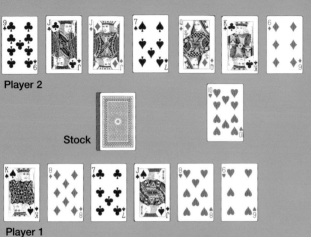

Player 2

Stock

Player 1

A player who cannot follow suit or match the previous card must pick up from the stock until he receives a playable card. Once the stock is used up, players with no playable card must 'pass' (lose their turn and wait for the next trick to be played).

The trick is won by the highest card of the suit led. The winner of a trick leads to the next trick. Tricks are put to one side as they do not have any scoring value.

Play continues until one player gets rid of all his cards. He shouts 'Boom!' and wins the game.

15

Go Fish *

Number of Players: *Two.*
How to Win: *By collecting more of the cards in the pack than your opponent.*

How to Do It:

Cut for dealer (highest card). Deal out seven cards, one at a time, to each player. Place the remaining cards (the stock) face down in the middle of the table.

The non-dealer begins by looking at his hand, and asking his opponent to hand over all the cards he has of a certain rank. For example, he might say: 'Please hand over all your 2s.' He must hold at least one card of this rank himself.

If the opponent has any 2s (or whatever rank is requested) he must hand them over. The first player may then ask again for another rank. If he doesn't have any, the opponent replies: 'Go fish'. The first player then picks up the top card from the stock. If it is the rank he asked for, he shows it, and is allowed to ask again for another rank. If it is not, it becomes the opponent's turn to ask for cards.

If the first player (top row) said: 'please hand over all your 2s', he would get two 2s from his opponent!

Stock

When a player has all four cards of the same rank, he places them face down on the table. When a player has used all the cards in his hand, he takes the top card of the stock as his next turn. The winner is the player who gains most sets of four.

Last Card *

Number of Players: Two.
How to Win: By making your opponent lose all his cards.

How to Do It:

1 Cut for dealer (ace is low). Dealer deals out ten cards to each player, one at a time. The next card is placed face up on the table to show the trump suit. The remaining cards are placed in a pile, face down, to form the stock.

2 The aim now is to win tricks by putting down the higher card. The non-dealer starts. The opponent then follows with a higher card of the same suit or a trump. Remember aces are low. The winner of each trick takes a card from the stock to add to his hand, and leads to the next trick.

3 One player will run out of cards – the other is the winner.

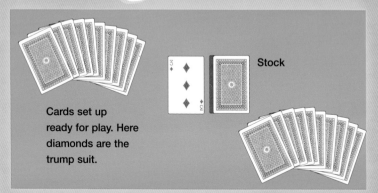

Stock

Cards set up ready for play. Here diamonds are the trump suit.

Gops *

Number of Players: Two.
How to Win: By capturing the greatest number of cards from the diamond suit.

How to Do It:

1 Divide your pack as follows: Take out all the hearts – they are not used in this game. Take the diamonds, shuffle them well, and place them in a packet face down between the two players.

2 Each player then takes either spades or clubs as his hand. It doesn't matter which, but they should not be mixed.

3 Turn the top diamond over and place it face up on the table. Now both players bid for the diamond, by choosing one of their cards and placing it face down on the table.

4 The players turn over their cards. The higher card (aces are low) wins the diamond. If the spade and club cards bid are of the same value, it is a tie, and neither player gets the diamond in this round. Another diamond is turned over and the bidding process is repeated. The winner of the second round gets both the diamonds. Once played, the black cards stay on the table; they cannot be reused.

5 The diamonds are turned over and bid for, until they have all been taken. If there is a tie on the last diamond, when there are no black cards left, roll a dice, or toss a coin for heads and tails.

Player 1

 Player 2 wins the
diamond with his
higher bid.

Scoring:
Method 1: The simplest way to score *Gops* is simply to count the number of diamonds gained by each player: the one with the most is the winner.

Method 2: Add the value of each player's diamonds, from 1 (ace) to 11 (jack), 12 (queen) to 13 (king). First player to reach or pass an agreed total – say 100 – is the winner.

Old Man's Bundle **

Number of Players: Two.
How to Win: By gaining the largest number of cards.

How to Do It:

1 Cut the pack to choose dealer (ace is low). The dealer deals four cards to each player, one at a time, and places another four face up on the table.

3 The bundles taken in by each player are placed before him in a face-up pile. If the opponent holds a card of the same value as the top card of the bundle, he can capture the bundle and take it to his side.

4 Each time the hands are played out, the players receive another four cards, but no more are dealt to the table.

5 When the pack is all used up, the player with the most cards is the winner.

2 The non-dealer goes first. He can choose to either 'take in' a card from the four on the table, by placing on it a card of the same rank from his hand. This starts a 'bundle' that belongs to him. Or, if he cannot make a bundle, he must 'trail' by placing one of his cards face up alongside the four on the table. This card can now be taken in by his opponent, if he has one of the same rank.

This player has taken in a card from the layout and started a bundle. If his opponent has a 7, he can capture it.

20

Pelmanism **

This game is sometimes called Memory – you'll see why.
Number of Players: Two.
How to Win: By having most tricks at the end of the game.

How to Do It:

1 Cut the cards to decide which player gets first turn (aces low; highest card wins). Lay out the whole pack face down on a table (or perhaps the floor), making sure each card is separate from its neighbours.

2 The first player turns over any two cards. If they are of the same rank (for example, two 3s), they form a pair and the player picks them up and lays them in front of him, face down.

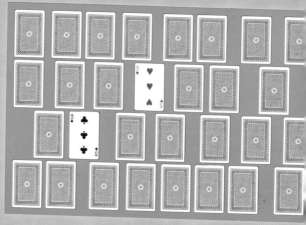

3 The same player turns up another two cards. When he turns over two that do not make a pair, he replaces them face down in their original positions. It is now the other player's turn. *Pelmanism* is all about remembering which card was where, so it is a great game for practising memory skills.

4 The game continues until all the cards have been paired. The winner is the player who has collected most pairs.

Knaves *

Number of Players: *Three.*
How to Win: *By winning the greatest number of tricks, without taking any jacks (knaves) in the process.*

1

How to Do It:
Use the 52-card pack and cut for dealer (ace is low). The dealer deals 17 cards to each player, turning over the last card to denote the trump suit.

2

The player to the dealer's left leads with any card. The other players must follow suit if they can; otherwise they play a trump. If they can't do either, they can play any card.

The highest card played wins the trick, and the winner leads to the next trick.

3

This continues until all cards are played. The skill in this game consists in getting rid of any jacks in your hand without using them to win a trick.

Scoring:
Players get one point for each trick they win, provided it does not contain a jack. If it does, players lose points as follows: jack of hearts – 4 points; diamonds – 3 points; clubs – 2 points; spades – 1 point.

If a player cannot follow suit, he can play a trump to win a trick.

Players lose points for each jack they collect, as shown above.

Pisha Pasha *

Number of Players: *Two.*
How to Win: *By having the greatest number of cards at the end of the game.*

How to Do It:
Cut for dealer (ace is high). Shuffle the pack and deal it into two face-down packets of 26.

Each player takes one of the packets. At the same time as each other, they turn over the top card from their piles until two cards of the same suit appear (for example, 6 and 8 of hearts).

The player who turned over the higher card (aces are high) picks up both turned-up cards and adds them to his packet.

Players continue to turn over cards from the face-down packets until they run out. The player with the most cards is the winner.

Slapjack *

Number of Players: *Two or more.*
How to Win: *By gaining all the cards.*

How to Do It:

1 Cut for dealer. Deal out the whole pack, one card at a time. Players do not look at their hands, but place them face down in a packet on the table.

2 Now, starting from the dealer's left, each player, one by one, turns up the top card of his packet and lays it face up in the centre of the table.

3 Everyone must be able to reach the centre of the table, because, when a jack is turned up, the first player to put his hand on top of the jack wins it (and the pile beneath it, if there is one). He puts these cards face down beneath his own pile; and play starts again, beginning with the player to the left of the person who turned up the jack.

4 When a player has won all the cards, the game is at an end. Players who have lost all their cards, drop out.
Note: Players use the same hand to turn cards and slap the jack.

Old Maid *

Number of players: *Two to five.*
How to Win: *By avoiding being left with the unpaired queen.*

How to Do It:

Use a 52-card pack. Cut for dealer (highest card). Take out one of the queens and deal out the remaining 51 cards (it doesn't matter if one player has an extra card).

Each player sorts his cards and puts aside, face down, all the cards that can be put into pairs, for example, two jacks, two 6s, etc. After each player has sorted his cards, the dealer offers his cards face down to the player on his left. The player chooses a card and quickly looks at it. If it makes a pair with a card already in his hand, he discards the pair. It is then his turn to present his cards, again face down, to the next player on the left.

Players continue to take it in turn to offer their cards on the table, face down, to the player on their left to select one.

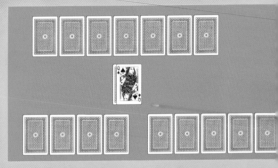

Eventually all the cards will be paired except for the one remaining queen. The player who is left with the 'old maid' loses the round.

Play continues for an agreed number of rounds, with the winner being the one to win the most rounds.

Snap *

Number of players: *Two to five.*
How to Win: *By collecting all the cards in the pack, leaving your opponent with none.*

How to Do It:

Use the 52-card pack. Cut to choose dealer; higher card wins. The dealer deals out half the pack to each player, one card at a time. Players keep their cards face down in a pile: they are not allowed to look at them or pick them up.

Snap!

The non-dealer turns over the top card of his pile and lays it face up. The dealer immediately turns over his top card and puts it directly on top of the first card, also face up. This goes on until one player puts down a card of the same rank as the last one. The first player to call 'Snap' on seeing it, wins all the face-up cards, which he adds to the bottom of his own pile.

He then turns over his top card, and play goes on in the same way until one player has won all the cards. The quicker players keep turning over their cards, the more fun this game will be.

27

Switch **

Also played as Eights (see Note).
Number of players: *Two to eight.*
How to Win: *To be first to put down all your cards.*

How to Do It:

Use the standard 52-card pack, or two packs if there are six or more players. Cut for dealer (highest card). Starting from his left, the dealer deals five cards to each player. (If there are only two playing, deal seven cards.)

The remaining cards are placed face down to form the stock, and the top card is turned up and placed alongside the stock, as the starter. If it is an ace, replace it in the middle of the stock pile and turn over the next card.

From the dealer's left, each player in turn plays a card on to the table, face up, making a row from the starter card. Each card played must be of equal rank or the same suit as the previous one. Aces are wild, and a player putting down an ace can call a new suit to follow. Any player who cannot put down a card must carry on drawing cards from the stock until he draws a playable one.

Scoring:

If one player has got rid of all his cards, each opponent awards him payment points according to the value of the cards he is left holding. Aces are 50 points, all court cards ten, other cards by their pip value. If the game ends in a block, all players count their hands, and the player with the lowest total collects from each opponent the difference between his score and theirs.

The game ends when one player has got rid of all his cards; or if no one can play a further card.

Each player must follow suit or put down a card of the same rank.

Stock

This player's cards add up to 37, which are awarded to the winner.

As the 8s are wild, this player's cards are worth 60 points to the winner.

In this game the 8s are wild. One player has got rid of all his cards, so there is a clear winner.

Note:

This game can also be played as *Eights,* when all the 8s are wild. The rules are the same, but in scoring, aces count for one point and 8s for 50. See also the game of *Crazy Eights* (on pages 34–35).

Games for

3

or more

players

Snip, Snap, Snorem *

Number of Players: *Three to eight.*
How to Win: *By being first to get rid of all your cards.*

How to Do It:

1 Choose a dealer. From his left, the dealer deals out the whole pack, one at a time. It doesn't matter if some players have extra cards.

2 The player on the dealer's left starts the game by putting a card face up on the table. Let's suppose it's a king. Play moves to the left. The next player with a king then lays it down, saying 'Snip.' The next player holding a king puts it down, saying 'Snap.' The player with the final king puts it down and says 'Snorem.'

3 If a player is unable to play a matching card, he says 'pass', and play moves to the next person on his left. If a player holds more than one king, he must play them one at a time. The player who puts down the fourth card of the rank then leads the card for the next group.

'Snip'   'Snap'   'Snorem'

4 The first player to put down all his cards is the winner, and the game is over.

Cheat! **

Number of players: *Three or more.*
How to Win: *By being first to get rid of all the cards in your hand.*

How to Do It:

1 Use the standard 52-card pack. Cut for dealer (highest card). Deal out the whole pack, one at a time.

2 The player to the dealer's left starts by placing, face down, one to four cards in the middle of the table. He should only put down cards of the same rank. He will then say, for example, 'here are three aces', but remember the name of the game – he might not be telling the truth about how many cards he has put down, their suit or their value!

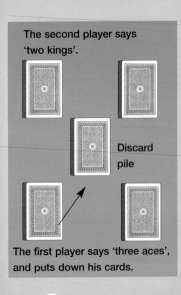

The second player says 'two kings'.

Discard pile

The first player says 'three aces', and puts down his cards.

3 If none of the other players challenges him by calling 'Cheat!', the next player to the left takes his turn, placing his cards face down on top of the cards already played, and saying what he is discarding.

4 Players should only put down cards of the same value or the next rank up as those just put down (ace if it was a king, 2 if it was an ace). But you never know when someone is cheating.

5 If an opposing player calls 'Cheat!' the last player must turn his discarded cards face up. If he was cheating, he has to pick up his own cards again, plus all the others (if any) in the discard pile. If he was not cheating, the caller must pick up all the cards in the pile.

6 The game goes on in this way until one player has successfully laid down all his cards.

The third player calls 'Cheat!'. The second player turns over his cards. As he was cheating (he put down a 10 and a king), he has to pick up all the cards.

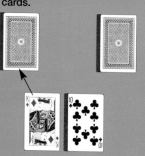

Crazy Eights **

Number of Players: *Can be played by two, but three to five is better.*
How to Win: *To be first to get rid of all one's cards, and to reach 500 points.*

How to Do It:

1 Use the standard 52-pack. Cut for dealer (highest card). Dealer deals seven cards to each player, one at a time, if it is a two-handed game; five if there are more than two players. The remaining cards are placed face down to form the stock. Turn the top card up to start the discard pile.

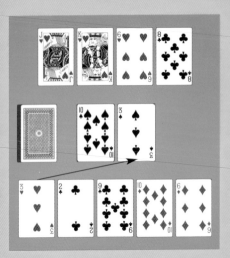

2 Starting on the dealer's left, the first player must put down a card of the same suit or of the same rank as the face-up card on the discard pile. For example, if it is 10 spades, a player may put down another spade or the 10 of a different suit. Now each player must match the card that has been put down before him.

3 If a player cannot play a matching card, he must pick up cards from the stock until he gets a card he can play. (Players are allowed to draw from the stock even if they can play.)

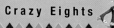

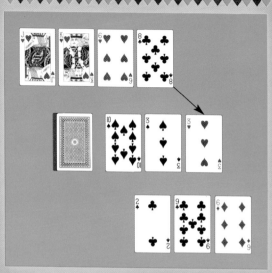

Scoring:
The winner of a round scores 100.

4 The four 8s are wild. An 8 can be played at any time, when it is a player's turn. An 8 can be called any suit of the player's choice. The next player has to follow the new suit or play another 8.

5 The first player to put down all his cards calls out 'Crazy eights!' and wins the round. If none of the players can get rid of all their cards, the round is won by the player with the fewest cards to the dealer's left. The first player to reach 500 points wins the game.

Variants: To make it more difficult, players can choose a rank (for example, a queen) and whenever a player puts down a queen, the next player has to miss a turn. Players could also agree that when an ace is played, the direction of play is reversed.

Knock-Out Whist **

Number of players: Three or more.
How to Win: By gaining the greatest number of tricks.

How to Do It:

1 Use the 52-card pack. Aces are high. Cut for dealer (highest card). The dealer then deals seven cards to each player. The rest of the cards are placed face down, and the top one is turned over to decide trumps for the first round.

2 The player to the dealer's left leads the first card. Players must follow suit if they can, otherwise they may play any card or trump.

3 In the second round, six cards are dealt (and five in the third round, down to one in the final round). The winner of a round decides what will be trumps for the next round, after the deal.

4 In the seventh round, when only one card is dealt to each player, the players cut for trumps, taking the suit of the highest card.

5 A player who does not take any tricks in any round is 'knocked out' and takes no more part in the game. However, the first player not to take a trick in a round is awarded the 'dog's chance'. He is dealt one card in the next round, and can play it to the trick of his choice. If he wins it, he is fully back in the game for the next round. If not, he's out.

Player 3

'dog's chance'

Player 2

Player 1

Winner from
previous round

In the second round, this winner should choose spades as the trump
suit. Player 3 has the 'dog's chance' to try to get back into the game,
after failing to win a trick in the previous round.

It is usually the player with the
greatest number of tricks that wins
the game. However, it can be won in
any round after the third if one
player takes all the tricks.

◆◆◆◆◆◆◆◆◆◆◆◆◆◆◆◆◆◆◆◆◆◆◆◆◆◆◆◆◆◆◆

Pip-Pip **

Number of Players: *Three to seven.*
How to Win: *By scoring points for changing the trump suit, and for capturing certain cards.*

How to Do It:

1 Use two standard 52-card packs, thoroughly shuffled together. Cut for dealer (highest card), and cut again to identify trumps. Dealer deals seven cards to each player and places the remainder face down as the stock.

2 The player on the dealer's left leads to the first trick. Other players must follow suit if they can, or play a trump, or discard from another suit. The trick is taken by the highest card of the suit led, or by the highest trump (see Scoring values). If two identical cards are played, the second beats the first.

3 The winner of a trick takes the top card from the stock and adds it to his hand, and other players, from his left, do the same. When there are not enough cards left in the stock to go round, no more cards are drawn, and hands are played until all cards are gone.

4 Changing trumps: Just before a card is led to a new trick, a player with a king and queen of the same suit (so long as it is not the trump suit) in his hand can turn that suit into trumps by saying 'Pip-pip', and laying the cards face down on the table. They continue to be playable as part of his hand. This also earns a bonus of 50 points.

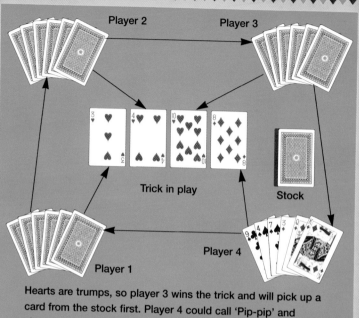

Hearts are trumps, so player 3 wins the trick and will pick up a card from the stock first. Player 4 could call 'Pip-pip' and change trumps to diamonds if he wished, because he has both the king and queen.

If two players call 'Pip-pip' before the same trick, both get 50 points, but the later call becomes trumps. A player can call 'Pip-pip' twice for the same suit, so long as he has both kings and both queens.

Scoring:

The only cards with scoring values are:
2s (known as deuces): 11; aces: 10; kings: 5; queens: 4; jacks: 3; all others: nil.
Each player adds up his card-score and his pipping score at the end of each round, and the highest score is the winner.

Games for

4

or more players

Fall Out *

Number of Players: *Four to six.*
How to Win: *By being the last player left in the game.*

How to Do It:

1 Shuffle the 52-card pack and cut for dealer (aces low). Turn over the top card to show the trump suit.

2 Dealer deals out four cards if there are four players; five each to five players, and six each to six players. The rest of the pack (the stock) is placed face down in the centre of the table.

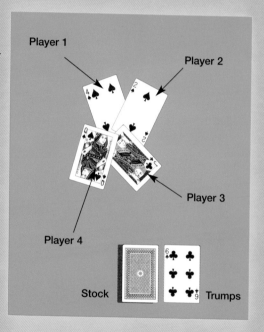

Player 1

Player 2

Player 3

Player 4

Stock

Trumps

3 The player on the dealer's left leads to the first trick. Players who cannot follow suit may trump, or discard (play a card of any other suit). The winner of the trick leads to the next trick, but first he takes the top card from the stock into his hand (without showing it to the others). As they run out of cards, players drop out of the game. The last player left is the winner.

Black Maria **

Also known as Black Lady, Calamity Jane and Hearts.
Number of Players: Four to seven.
How to Win: By obtaining the lowest score.

How to Do It:

1 Cut the pack to select a dealer (highest score: ace is low). If there are five players, remove two 2s from the pack; six players, take out all four 2s; seven players, remove three 2s. This is to ensure that each player is dealt an equal number of cards. Deal out the whole pack.

2 The object of the game is to avoid winning tricks containing the queen of spades or any hearts (but see Step 4).

Once each player has looked at his hand, he chooses three cards and passes them, face down, to the player on his left. Cards must be discarded before players pick up the three cards from their neighbour.

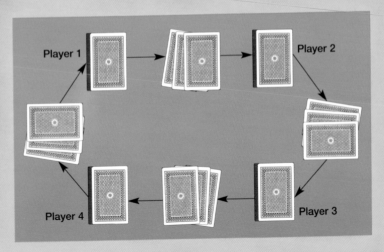

Player 1

Player 2

Player 3

Player 4

3 There is no trump suit. The player on the dealer's left leads a card. Other players in turn must follow suit, if they can. The highest card (of the suit led) wins the trick. If players cannot follow suit, they can play any card.

4 As the aim of this game is to get the lowest score, players should avoid winning tricks that contain any cards of the heart suit and the queen of spades – Black Maria. These cards have certain values (see table below), and remember the points will count against the players. However, if a player takes <u>all</u> the hearts plus Black Maria, none of the players score in that round.

Card values:

Queen of spades (Black Maria): 13
Any card from the heart suit: 1
All other cards: 0

Bonus Card:

By agreement with the other players, you can nominate one card as a 'bonus card'. This is usually the jack of diamonds, and if you end up with it, you can deduct ten points from your score. Play continues until one player reaches an agreed total such as 150. The winner is the player with the lowest score.

◆◆◆◆◆◆◆◆◆◆◆◆◆◆◆◆◆◆◆◆◆◆◆◆◆◆◆◆

Casino **

Number of Players: *Can be played by two, three or four, each on his own; but it is a fun game to play with a partner, if there are four of you.*

How to Win: *To score the highest number of points by capturing cards from the layout and your opponents.*

How to Do It:

Partners sit facing each other. Choose a dealer, who deals two cards, face down, to each other player, places two cards face up on the table, and deals himself two, face down. He repeats, this until each player has four cards, and there are four face-up cards (the layout). The remaining cards (the stock) are put aside, face down. In *Casino*, aces are low and court cards have no value at all. Values therefore go from 1 (ace) to 10.

Scoring:

For capturing most cards: 3
For capturing 10 diamonds: 2
For capturing most spades: 1
For capturing 2 spades: 1
For each ace captured: 1
For each sweep (all the layout captured at once): 1

Usually the game is played to 21 points. If a player thinks that his side has reached that number, he calls 'Out!'. Play stops and points are counted. If the player was right, his team wins. If he got it wrong, his team loses. Alternatively, play can continue until the sixth deal. Points are then counted, and the player or team with the highest total wins.

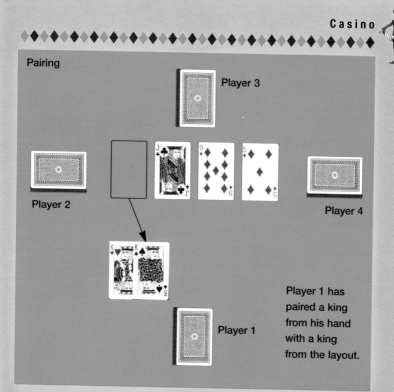

Pairing

Player 3

Player 2

Player 4

Player 1

Player 1 has paired a king from his hand with a king from the layout.

Play starts with the player to the dealer's left. He must try to capture a card, or cards, from the table, by matching their value with cards already in his hand. The simplest way to do this is **Pairing.** For example, if a player holds the king of hearts, he can pick up the king of spades from the layout. Court cards can capture only one card, but number cards can capture two or three of the same rank. Captured cards are kept in a face-down pile in front of each player. If no card can be matched, a player must **Trail** (see step 7).

A player could also **Combine**. For example, he could pick up a 3 and an ace, and match their total of 4 to a 4 in his hand. This is called **Combining**. It is possible for a single card to capture all four from the layout if it matches their combined value: for example, a 7 can capture a 3, a 2 and two aces.

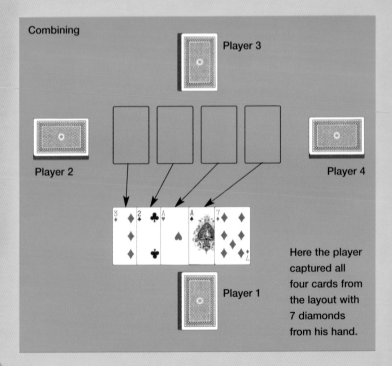

Combining

Player 3

Player 2

Player 4

Player 1

Here the player captured all four cards from the layout with 7 diamonds from his hand.

46

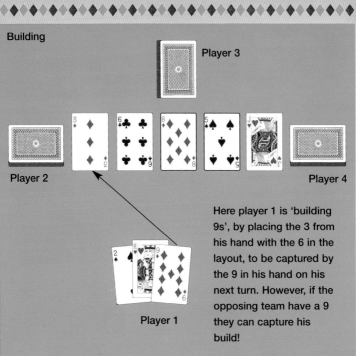

Building

Player 3

Player 2

Player 4

Here player 1 is 'building 9s', by placing the 3 from his hand with the 6 in the layout, to be captured by the 9 in his hand on his next turn. However, if the opposing team have a 9 they can capture his build!

Player 1

Another option, important in the partnership game, is **Building**. Here the player adds a card to the layout with the aim of capturing cards on his next turn – or giving his partner a chance to do so. For example, if the player has a 9 and a 3 in his hand, and sees a 6 on the table, he can add the 3 from his hand to the 6, and say 'building 9s.' Players cannot build and take in the same turn because only one card may be played at each turn. On his next turn he can capture both cards with his 9, but if a player from the opposing partnership has a 9, they could capture the build. Any player can have more than one build going on at the same time.

47

A player must not leave a build unless he has a card in his hand that can take it. On his next turn he must take the build, duplicate or increase it, as described below.

Duplicating: If a player had two 9s in his hand, after building the 6 and 3, he could put down one of the 9s in his next turn; then take the build with the other 9 in his third turn.

Builds can also be increased. Suppose that one player has laid a 4 from his hand on a 5 on the table and called 'building 9'. An opposing player has an ace and a 10. He can add the ace to the build and say 'building 10'. Players are allowed to increase builds of their own in the same way. It is only possible to increase a single build, not a duplicated one. A player must use a card from his hand to increase the build.

If a player cannot pair, combine or build, he has no choice but to **trail** a card, in the hope that his partner can use it. **Trailing** is simply adding an extra card from your hand to the layout.

After the last card of the sixth deal is played, any cards left on the table at this point go to the side which made the last capture.

Players look through their captured cards and add up their scores, as described on page 44.

If player 3 also holds a 10, he could recapture the build for his team.

Player 2 has added an ace (worth 1 point) and calls 'Building 10s!'. He hopes to capture the build with his 10 next turn.

Player 1 is building 9s by adding a 4 to the 5 on the table.

Player 4

Three-Card Brag **

Number of Players: *Four (three to six is possible).*
How to Win: *By winning the most rounds with the best combination of cards.*

How to Do It:

Use the standard 52-card pack. Cut for dealer (highest card). Dealer then deals three cards to each player.

If no one has a set (as in Step 2), then the highest card wins the round, starting with the ace, and going down to 2. If more than one player has an ace, the value of the other cards is taken into consideration. Ace, king, 3 will beat ace, queen, jack. Ten, 7, 5 will beat 10, 7, 4.

The wild cards: To make the game more interesting, three cards can be chosen as 'wild' (sometimes called the 'braggers'). In order of rank they are: the ace of diamonds, jack of clubs, and 9 diamonds. They can be used in place of other cards to make winning combinations.

Each player puts his cards, face up, on the table. The player with the best combination of cards wins the round.

Hand values (highest first)

Three aces (aces are high)
Three kings
Three queens – and so on down to three 2s.
Two aces plus another card
Two kings plus another card
Two queens plus another card – and so on down to two 2s and another card.
(If two players have a pair of cards of the same value, then the player with the higher-value singleton wins. If the singletons are also of the same value, the player nearest the dealer's left wins).

Scoring:

Agree in advance how many hands to play – let's say nine, for example. Then set out nine counters or tokens on the table as the 'pool'. At the end of each round the winning player takes a token. The winner is the player with most tokens at the end of the game.

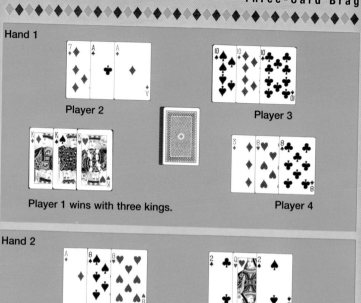

Hand 1

Player 2

Player 3

Player 1 wins with three kings.

Player 4

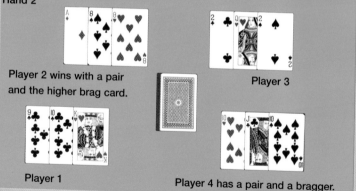

Hand 2

Player 2 wins with a pair and the higher brag card.

Player 3

Player 1

Player 4 has a pair and a bragger.

However, a natural combination will always beat a brag combination of the same value. For example, two kings and any other card will beat two kings plus a bragger. When there is more than one brag hand, the higher-value bragger will win – a 6 plus the ace of diamonds will beat another 6 plus the jack of clubs.

◆◆◆◆◆◆◆◆◆◆◆◆◆◆◆◆◆◆◆◆◆◆◆◆◆◆◆◆◆◆◆

Twenty-Nine*

Number of players: *Four, playing as two sets of partners.*
How to Win: *By gaining the most tricks – each trick adding up to 29 points.*

How to Do it:

1 Players should sit round the four sides of the table, with partners facing each other. Choose a dealer, who deals out 13 cards to each player, one card at a time.

2 Play is started by the player to the dealer's left, who places a card face up on the table.

3 Each player in turn puts down a card. This continues until a player puts down a card that brings the value of all the face-up cards to 29 (for example, 2, 5, 1, 1, 10, 8, 1, 1). The player who puts down the final card that achieves the 29 wins the trick for his team.

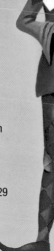

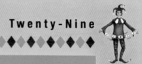

Player 3

Player 2

Player 4

Player 1

Player 1 led by putting down 9 hearts. Player 2 put down 8 clubs. The total is now 17, Player 3 wants his partner (player 1) to win the trick. He puts down a queen, worth only one point, thereby making it impossible for player 4 to reach 29. Player 1 has a good chance of reaching 29 with one of his cards.

The next player to his left then leads another card and so play goes on. If a player cannot put down a card without going over 29, he has to pass. If the very last trick fails to reach 29, it is ignored.

Scoring in Twenty-Nine:
Ace, king, queen, jack are all worth a single point. Other cards according to their pip value, from 10 to 2.

Great
Party Games
for Larger Numbers

Menagerie *

Number of Players: Between three and 13 – a good party game.
How to Win: By ending up with everyone else's cards.

How to Do It:

1 Use a 52-card pack. A dealer is chosen, and all the cards are dealt out. Each player takes the name of a different wild animal.

2 Each player puts his packet of cards face down in front of him, without looking at them.

3 Starting from the dealer's left, each player turns over one card from his packet. Watch the cards carefully. If two players turn over a card of the same rank, the first player to call out the other's animal name wins the other's face-up cards, and takes them into his own packet.

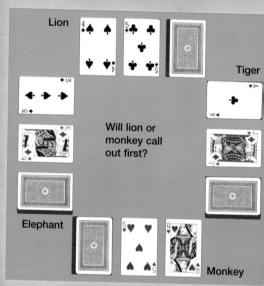

Lion

Tiger

Will lion or monkey call out first?

Elephant

Monkey

4 Play goes on until another pair are exposed. When a player has turned all his cards face up, he turns the packet over and starts again. Eventually, one player will get all the cards and win the game.

Chase the Ace *

Number of Players: *Two or more.*
How to Win: *Be the last player left in the game.*
You will need: *Three counters for each player (different colours if possible).*
Why is it called this? Because any ace gets passed round the table like a hot potato!

How to Do It:

1 Choose a dealer. The dealer shuffles and cuts the pack, then deals out a single card to each player, face down.

2 Now each player looks at his hand. The player with the lowest card (aces are low) will lose the round. Each player has to decide whether his card is high enough to keep him in the game. If the player thinks it is, he will say 'Stand' (stick with his card). If a player thinks his card is too low, he will say 'Exchange,' and pass the card, face down, to the player on his left, who must accept it and give him his card in return. This process continues round the table until play comes back to the dealer.

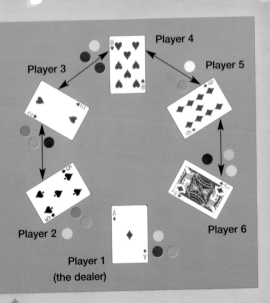

Player 4

Player 5

Player 3

Player 2

Player 6

Player 1
(the dealer)

56

3 If the dealer is dissatisfied with his card, he replaces it at the bottom of the pack and draws the top card instead.

4 All players show their cards. The player with the lowest card puts one of his counters into the centre.

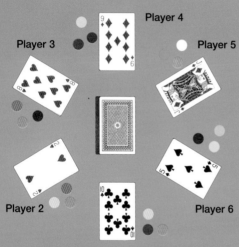

Player 4

Player 3

Player 5

Player 2

Player 6

Player 1 (the dealer) replaced his ace and drew the 10 clubs, so player 2 loses the round.

5 Cards are then reshuffled and redealt, and the same process is repeated. When a player loses all three counters, he drops out. If two or more players tie for lowest card, each pays a counter.

Special rule:
If you are dealt a king, you neither stand nor exchange. Place your card face up in front of you, and relax for the rest of the round.

My Bird Sings *

Number of Players: *Three to seven.*
How to Win: *By being the first to have a complete set of cards of the same suit.*

How to Do It:

1 For three players, use a pack of 21 cards, making sure there are seven (in a sequence) of three of the suits. For four players, use 28 cards, again making sure there are seven cards in a sequence. For more than four players, use a standard 52-card pack. Choose a dealer, who deals out seven cards, one at a time, to each player.

2 Put aside any remaining cards. Each player looks at his hand and chooses a card to pass to the player on his left.

3 Players pick up the card that h been passed to them. If a play has seven cards of the same s he calls out 'My Bird Sings!' a wins the round. If not, the process of putting down and picking up continues until a player does get a set of seven. If a player calls out incorrectly, there is a penalty: he must squawk 'cock-a-doodle-do' an pretend to flap his wings! Ther play begins again.

4 The first player to cal 'My bird sings!' four times, is the winner.

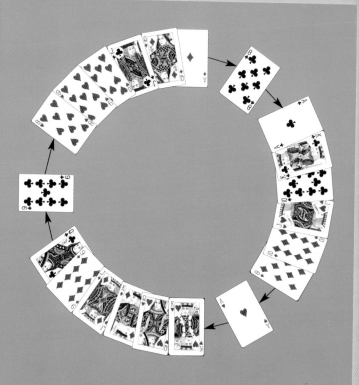

Players must continue to discard from their hands
and pick up from their neighbours until someone
shouts out 'My bird sings'.

◆◆◆◆◆◆◆◆◆◆◆◆◆◆◆◆◆◆◆◆◆◆◆◆◆◆◆

Pig *

Number of players: *Four to 13.*
How to Win: *By being first to get a matching set of cards in the last hand.*

How to Do it:

1 Count the number of players (13 is the maximum), and prepare sets of cards accordingly. For 13 use all 52 cards. For ten you need 40 cards (ten matching sets of four: you could eliminate all cards from 5 to 2); for five players you need 20 cards (five sets of four). Once you have the right number of sets, shuffle them thoroughly.

2 Choose a dealer, who deals four cards to each player.

3 Starting with the player on the dealer's left, each player chooses a card from his hand and passes it, face down, to his neighbour on the left. Cards continue to be passed like this until the first person to find he has four of a kind in his hand lays them face up on the table, and gives a clear agreed signal. This might be tapping the table, or grunting.

4 All other players must quickly notice this and lay down their cards and give the same signal – the last to do so is the pig.

You can play *Pig* as an elimination game, with the pig dropping out as each hand is played, until only two players are left.

When a player gets four of a kind, he must lay them down and make the signal. All the other players must follow the signal.

Words Used in Card Play

Ace High: Ace is top scoring card.

Ace Low: Ace is lowest scoring card.

Court Cards: Kings, queens and jacks.

Deal: Passing out cards to players. Most deals are one card at a time to each player, going from left to right but this can vary according to the game.

Deck: Another word for the pack.

Discard: In some games, to play a card of no value in the game, when the player cannot follow suit or play a trump. In other games, to play a card to the waste pile.

Flush: A set of cards all of the same suit.

Follow Suit: To play a card of the same suit as the first card played in a trick.

Hand: The cards held by a player at any point during the game. It can also be any cards which have not been dealt out (also called the stock).

Honour Cards: Ace, king, queen and jack of the trump suit.

Lead: Being first player to set down a card. Also the card played first (lead card).

Meld: a set of three or more of a kind, e.g. either all kings, or all hearts (but these must be in sequence of pip value with no gaps).

Number Card: Card of any value between 10 and 2.

Pack: The full set of 52 cards (or 53 with one joker, 54 with two jokers). Also known as a deck.

Packet: Set of cards that is less than a full pack.

Pair: Two cards of the same kind, e.g. two 2s.

Pass: To miss a turn.

Pip Value: The number on a number card (e.g. a 9 has nine pips).

Play: To play a card is to take it from your hand and use it in the game.

Rank: The value of a card. For example, two 9s are of the same rank, as are two kings.

Round: This is complete once each player has played his cards in any trick.

Sequence: The order in which the cards run, from high to low, or the other way round.

Singleton: A single card of any suit.

Stock: The cards remaining after dealing, sometimes also called the hand.

Trick: The cards played by all the players in a round, one from each.

Trumps: Cards of a chosen suit that outrank (and therefore beat) all cards in all other suits during the game. Trumping is playing a trump card.

Wild Card: A card which a player can use to represent any other card (within the rules of the game).

63

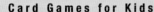
Index of Games